Google Classroom for Teachers (2020 and Beyond)

A User Guide for Beginners to Master the Use of Google Classroom to Provide Students With an Engaging and Fun Virtual Distance Learning

By

Chris Button

Disclaimer

This publication is designed to provide competent and reliable information regarding the subject matter covered. However, the views expressed in this publication are those of the author, and should not be taken as expert instruction or official advice from Google. The reader is responsible for his or her own actions.

The author hereby disclaims any responsibility or liability whatsoever that is incurred from the use or application of the contents of this publication by the purchaser or reader.

Table of Contents

Introduction

Technology has evolved.

Once, learning could only be done in person. For a person to learn, he had to move over to a physical location to meet an instructor, coach, or teacher. These learning centers could be physical schools or other environments where specific learning tools had been made available. This proved to be stressful; on the part of the teachers as well as the students.

One of the major challenges that were associated with the physical mode of learning was the fact that teachers were not really able to reach out to their students and effect the kind of change they wanted to see their children get. Students learn at different rates. For some, they are able to pick up concepts as the teacher is teaching, while others have to go over what is taught again and again for it to stick. The first category of students may not have had a lot of trouble with the physical mode of learning because all they had to do was stay in class and follow along, but it could not be said that the same was the case for the other kind of students.

The inability of students to have access to their teachers and vice versa placed a dampening on the learning process. So, teachers had to teach their students to the best of their abilities, in the hope that they understood what they learned in class. If it turned out that the student did not quite understand what was taught, he had to wait for when next he saw his teacher (maybe at school, or when they congregated again) to ask questions and gain clarity in those areas he was confused.

This, in a nutshell, was one of the major challenges that were experienced by teachers when all that was available was the physical system of learning.

In a bid to make life better for all that were involved, technology morphed to include cloud-based learning. Under these conditions, students had an advantage because they began to have access to more tools that were necessary for their academic success. Books, resources and learning materials began to be hosted online so that even when a student was unable to understand what his teacher taught, he could go back and source the internet for more materials and structured knowledge to help him understand better.

Taking it a step further, there came the introduction of more advanced Learning Management systems. These started becoming mainstream in the early 2000s and they allowed the learning process to become even better. This was because they contained extra tools and features that allowed teachers and instructors to create valuable training content for their students, administer these trainings and track their students' progress as they learned. With the advent of these technology-driven solutions, learning became much easier. However, recent events have shown that these are not just enough.

With the recent events happening around the world and the sudden shift of attention to the online and virtual space, the need for education and learning to be digitized has been reiterated again. The need for continuous learning, coupled with the unlimited power of the internet, drove companies and software developers to begin to look for even more innovative ways of learning. The innovations that have followed since then have been remarkable because they have greatly enhanced the learning process for students and they have also made the teaching experience for teachers much better.

This book is centered on one of these innovations that have enhanced the teaching and learning experience –

the Google Classroom. Google Classroom is a virtual classroom. It is a web-service (internet-based service) that was developed by Google Corporation. It is meant for schools and it is aimed at simplifying the creation, distribution, grading and tracking of assignments, among many others. In a nutshell, it is a collaboration tool for teachers and students. With it, teachers can create an online classroom, invite students to the classroom and simulate a physical learning environment with all the perks that come with it. One of the major advantages that come with making use of this tool is that it allows for teachers to be able to interact with their students in real-time as they have conversations about assignments given, review topics taught and using this tool, teachers can also be able to track their student's progress seamlessly.

In this book, we are going to take a deep look at the inner workings of this tool. In the end, you would have learned;

- The basics of Google Classroom.
- A quick tour of the tool. You will be put through how to navigate the app as a teacher and how to

make good use of all its features to get the best out of it for you and for your students.

- How to communicate with your students to keep up with their progress in class and how to keep in touch with their parents because they, too, deserve to be in the loop as to the progress of their children.
- How to make use of Google Meet to create live video classes. These classes are where you get to interact with your students in real-time, even though they are not with you physically.
- Other cool applications and extensions that you can incorporate into the Google Classroom to make the most out of this tool.

And a whole lot more.

The Google Classroom is an amazing tool for you to use as a teacher because it allows you flexibility and also makes the teaching process fun for you, and also exciting for your students. Even if you are yet to make use of the application, you will find all the knowledge you will need in this book as you will get to see the benefits and perks of incorporating this tool into your teaching efforts.

If you are ready to step up your teaching game, then let us get right into it.

Chapter 1

ABC of Google Classroom

What is Google Classroom

Google Classroom is a free web-based platform that integrates your G Suite for Education account with all your G Suite services, including Google Docs, Gmail and Google calendar. Classroom saves time and paper, and makes it easier to create classes, distribute assignments, communicate with students and stay organized.

With the tool, you can carry out a lot of activities, just like you can do with your physical classroom. This tool incorporates these features and makes distance learning fun and engaging for teachers and the students alike.

Around the world, tens of millions of teachers and students across thousands of schools have been able to incorporate the Google Classroom tool into their learning experience. The result of this is that there has been a drastic change in the way teachers teach and the way students learn. This cloud-based tool enhances the chances of better learning, access to a lot of tools that aid the teaching and learning process (due to the power of the internet), and it gives the leverage for all learning parties to co-exist in a collaborative way to make sure that the process is as seamless as it can get. The Google Classroom tool is one of the most popular EdTech tools around the world; this a proof of its efficiency and the results that have been obtained by those who have used it.

To present this software in a way that is more basic, Google Classroom is a tool that incorporates all of Google's G Suite tools for teachers and students. With it, teachers can keep their digital instructional materials in a way that is organized, share these materials with their students for easy learning, and interact with their students. Amongst many things, Google Classroom is a lifesaver because it takes distance learning to a new level of fun. Students do not have to congregate around a teacher to learn, neither do they have to be left to figure themselves out over a digital learning material like a course or some voluminous text they stumbled into online. With this tool, the teacher controls the classroom environment, but the students still get to have almost-uninterrupted access to their instructor – no matter where they are in the world.

By the end of 2018, Google Classroom became available as an additional service to companies that are G Suite basic. It was also made available to businesses and enterprise customers.

Who is Google Classroom For?

Google Classroom is for;

- Teachers (grade school, middle school, and high school teachers alike).
- Lecturers and instructors in universities and colleges.
- Coaches.
- Consultants.
- Organizations.
- Families.
- Homeschoolers, etc.

Google Classroom can be used by anyone who is in the position to teach/train people in a particular area. It comes as a free service for those who have a personal Google account. In addition to this, Google Classroom is also free for use for corporations and organizations that use G Suite for education or for Nonprofits.

When set up for a school, the teachers and students of that school can access their virtual classroom through a google account provided by their school. Even when it is to be used in the corporate setting, employees of the corporation and their trainers can access their classrooms using the account that has been provided for the corporation by Google. If you are a trainer or a teacher of any sort, and you have been looking for an effective way to congregate your students from all parts of the world without physical collaboration, then you may need to give this software a try.

Key Features of Google Classroom

Since the launch of this tool, it has gained grounds and has come to be the go-to option for many teachers, instructors and trainers. This is not only a result of the meticulousness that was exhibited by the manufactures in creating this tool, but also due to the global crises that prompted teachers and trainers to seek out a means of providing an online, virutual learning. There are a few reasons why it stands out amongst other tools in the same category, and these are what makes the Google Classroom the go-to choice for millions of teachers and students.

In this section of the book, we will be looking at a few of these reasons (what makes this tool something you should incorporate into your teaching efforts).

Here are a few key features of Google Classroom.

1. Virtual Discussions

Remember we said that one of the major reasons while the Google Classroom is a great tool for learning is that it encourages distance learning in real time. This implies that with this tool, administrators or teachers can congregate students from all over the world in a virtual place, and get them to learn at the same time. The 'virtual discussions' tool is what makes this possible.

With this feature, teachers can invite their students into the classroom, permit them to answer questions, respond to classmates and also initiate conversations that can lead to more learning in class. This feature is made possible by the integration of the Google Docs tool, which is a tool that already allows for collaboration in the creation of written documents. With Google Docs, you can create a document that other people can interact with by making comments on specific parts of the document, and when you allow them to, they can even make edits that can be tracked by the person who created the document in the first place. With the features of this tool, teachers and students can have a more improved way of communicating with themselves as the learning process goes on. To give the teacher control over the class as it should be, Google included a feature in the classroom that allows teachers to mute students and/or unmute them when the demand arises.

2. Assignments

Classes are really not complete until the students have the opportunity of practicing what they have learned. With this in mind, the 'assignments' feature was incorporated into this tool. With this feature, teachers can create assignments that their students can work on and submit to them through the platform. Using learning and data collection materials like Youtube videos or other instructional videos hosted on other platforms, survey forms or digital books (pdfs), teachers can create and assign projects to each of their students. With this tool, the teacher can choose if he wants the student to see the assignment immediately or he can choose to schedule the assignment for the student to receive it and start working on it much later on.

3. Customizable Grading System

This is another feature that makes the classroom an amazing tool for many teachers and students alike. On this platform, teachers can create a customized grade system and different grade categories. If the students will be seeing their overall grades at the end of the learning season, the teacher has the option of choosing from the following grading options;

A. No overall grade; the teacher may choose to refrain from grading the students at the end of the learning system. If he chooses to do this, no grading system will be activated for that specific classroom.

B. Total points grading; with this option, the teacher allow the system to divide the total points that students earn by the maximum points that could have been earned. The result is what the student sees at the end of the learning period.

C. Weighted by category grading; In this grading system, every grade category is assigned a weight. Afterwards, the average score of each category is calculated and multiplied by the grade weight. The result of this calculation is the overall grade out of 100%.

With or without displaying the final grades of students after a learning season, the teacher is still able to keep track of his students' progress and these insights are what he uses to track whether or not the students are doing well.

4. Announcements

Just like a teacher is able to pass across a body of knowledge that is relevant to his students in a physical class, Google Classroom allows the teacher to be able to make announcements too. Announcements are usually updates that the teacher gives his students (and most times, they are neither classes nor assignments). Announcements are usually notices about classes, deadlines, how to do things that are related with the learning season or the courses being learned in the classroom and every other related information.

In the Google Classroom scenario, announcements are made as dedicated posts and the teacher controls what happens to the announcements like the replies or the comments that are made by students under them.

5. Live Classes

This is one of the latest improvements/upgrades to the software. This is made possible by the Google Meet feature and with it, teachers can be able to deliver a real-time class to their students. With this feature, up to 250 people can be a part of the Hangout call and up to a million people can live-stream the class from any part of the world. This potentially and exponentially increases the reach of the teachers and the amount of work they would have done trying to teach these numbers of people in smaller physical groups is reduced dramatically.

Another perk of this feature is that these live-classes can be recorded by the teacher so that those who were not able to follow during the live sessions can have access to the recordings and still be at par with other students. With these features, it is almost impossible for a student to be absent from class for a reason and completely miss out on what was taught.

6. The Gradebook Beta feature was introduced in an updated version of the Google Classroom app which was released in 2018. This feature allows the teacher to view, edit and instantly share grades using the

newly-introduced grades page. The grades page is a feature that allows the teacher to publish grades of his students on one page.

7. Classroom customization features allows the teacher to set up the classroom using the school's logo and preferred colors. Also, this tool allows rearranging and presenting the class in a new way to be done easily. With just a few clicks of some buttons, the teacher can rearrange his class in a way that allows for the best learning experience.

8. There are some other features that make this tool amazing for the online classroom learning experience. They include the features that allow the teacher some control over the academic work of the students, and they include;

- Reusing assignments, tests and class work for future purposes.
- Adding content like PDFs, videos, form surveys, etc. to assignments.
- Exporting grades to Google sheets so that they can be preserved in a way that is meaningful and easily understandable by the teacher.

There are still some other features of this tool, but these seem to be the most remarkable.

What Devices Does Google Classroom Support?

The Google Classroom app is available for the android and iOS platforms. Android devices and apple devices (including phones and tablets) are suitable for the classroom software. This application is also available for the Chrome-based devices (devices that use a Chrome OS) like Chromebooks. If you are looking to access the software using a Chromebook, you do not need to install the application because it comes pre-installed. Currently, the classroom application is not available for Windows mobile devices.

Benefits of Google Classroom

There are a ton of benefits you can get from the Google Classroom tool as a teacher, school owner, business person, or someone that has to virtually congregate people in a classroom setting. Here are a few of them;

1. This tool is easy to use and can be accessed from every device. It comes with an interface that is not complicated, and even if you are yet to use it, it does not take a lot for you to get the hang of the tool. Since it can be accessed from the Chrome app, you can access it by making use of the web version, which is accessible by all devices that have the Chrome application installed.

2. This tool is for everyone. Previously, we made a list of those that can make use of the Google Classroom. If you have a business where you teach people in a structured and highly-organized way without having to think of bringing them together in a physical place, this software is a lifesaver for your needs. Even if you are an educator or teacher, you are not prevented from joining a classroom as a student. What this implies is that your institution can create a classroom for the teachers that work in it, and in this classroom, you get to interact amongst yourselves, get trained also and have all the features of the classroom tool at your disposal. This can also come in handy to make sure that you are better equipped to give your students the best experience possible.

3. Effective communication and real-time sharing. The Google Classroom provides you with a lot of tools to be able to interact with your students and also get feedback from them. For example, in the live stream feature, the teacher is able to teach a lot of students and also get feedback from them immediately. With other incorporated tools and features like Google Docs, documents that are created are backed up online immediately and can be shared with an unlimited number of people. These people can give feedback as comments in the document (and all these comments can be tracked by all of those that have access to the document), or if the creator so chooses, he can allow for all of them to have access to make edits where they think is necessary. This is great as it fosters collaboration within projects and makes sure that the groups can work together to achieve whatever it is that they want to achieve.

4. Makes it easier and faster for the teacher to track assignments. All it takes is a click of the button, and all the students in a classroom can have access to the assignment that their teacher has created for them. The Google Classroom has features that allows the teacher to publish assignments without having to break into a sweat. He can also monitor the student's

progress in real-time (so that he can know who has completed his assignments, is in the process of doing, or has not even done his own), grade assignments easily and offer feedback to students as a group or individually almost immediately. On the other hand, students can submit assignments without having to go through rigorous processes and if they need the attention of their teacher, all they need to do is reach out for and grab it almost immediately.

5. Using this tool, there is no need for paper. Everything here is done over the cloud; learning materials are digital for example, PDFs, class meetings are done over the cloud and the students can even take notes using a digital platform or tool like Google Docs. This rules out the discomfort that comes with having to deal with big textbooks and the fear that comes with having to grade a ton of books per day. This also takes away the stress that comes from losing a learner's work, as everything is digital and cloud-based. If anything is lost, it can be regained within a jiffy.

6. Although this software allows for learners to learn in a beautiful and befitting environment, the instructor

still has control over the classroom. This is seen in the little features that are available in this tool, including the ability of the instructor to manage comments and reactions, mute/unmute learners, and other features available.

Top Reasons Google Classroom is a Must-Have

Why do you really need this tool, you may be asking yourself. Well, here's why you need it;

1. The top reason is because of the fact that the world is taking the digital turn. Now, more than ever before, you need to be able to take your career as an instructor beyond physical locations. With this tool, you can congregate several students and have them learn at the same time, no matter where in the world they are.

   This has solved the problem of physical distance and geographical barriers.

2. The tool is super easy to use. When you take a look at this tool as against many other Learning Management Systems out there, you will discover that it is really simple to make use of this tool as an

educator or a learner. Setting up and managing classrooms does not take much experience and with the right knowledge, even a newbie can get it done almost immediately.

3. It is a cost-effective way of training learners. Since this software is paperless, you can save the cost of printing and copying, channeling those funds to other areas of your venture. Also, not having to deal with papers is environmentally safe since it prevents the release of pollution that comes with littered and wasted papers.

4. With this tool, learners get to learn how to better collaborate amongst themselves. Classroom brings people from wherever they are to congregate in one place so they can learn from themselves. Because of this, and the fact that there are a lot of tools in this platform that fosters the practice of communal learning and access to the same tools, this software is a great way for the learners to begin to develop their team skills and their collaboration abilities.

5. This is the future of learning. With the advent of distance policies that are being enacted in various sectors of society, distance learning will soon be a

go-to solution in the area of education. Presently, many colleges do not expect their students to print out their seven-page essays, rather they are encouraged to submit them as soft documents (digital copies of the documents). This, alongside the ease of access that comes with this learning structure makes it one of the pioneer tools of the future of learning.

6. It is easy for the teacher to get feedback from the students instantly. One of the major benefits of making use of this tool is that it allows teachers to be able to interact with their students in real-time. To take this further, teachers can track their students' progress and make sure that they are getting the best out of the learning experience. By embedding forms into the learning tools, the teacher can request feedback on different sections and materials used in the training sessions and with this feedback, he can make better adjustments and serve the students in ways that are most conducive to them all.

7. Another reason why the Google Classroom is a must-have tool is because the developers are constantly updating it, tweaking it and making sure that better versions that have more functionalities

are released every time. The best part is that Google has the feature that allows the users of the application to send feedback. With these responses they get from people that are making use of the Google Classroom, they are able to optimize the experiences and make sure that future versions end up being better that the older versions. This implies that the tool can only get better as time unfolds.

Chapter 2

Getting Started with Google Classroom

Teacher's Guide

Accessing Google Classroom

Accessing the classroom is very easy. Even as a beginner, you can get started with accessing and making use of it. All you need to do is follow the outlined steps;

1. Determine whether or not your device is compatible with the classroom application. Earlier on, we made a list of all the devices and platforms that can allow you to make use of the application. If your operating system is not compatible with the classroom app, it means that you will not be able to make use of it on your device. This, however, does not mean that you will not be able to have access to the classroom. If you have the Chrome browser installed on your device, you will still be able to access the classroom.

2. If you are using an android device, visit the play store. On the play store, find and install the Google Classroom app.

3. If you are using an iOS device, visit the iOS app store. On the app store, find and install the Google Classroom app. Note, however, that for you to be able to access the latest version of the classroom app on this platform, you need to have a device with an operating system – iOS 11 or later.

4. If you are using a device owned by your school, or the school has the account you would like to log in to, you may have to contact your administrator for access and login details.

Now that you have installed the application on your device, it is time for you to sign up for the service (if you haven't opened an account already). The sign-up process is easy. All you need to do is;

1. Visit classroom.google.com
2. On the home page, you will be required to add your G suite email address. Once you have done this, hit the continue button which is directly under the place where you have entered your email address.

3. You will be taken to a page where you can create a new class, or join your first class. This is what it looks like.

Creating a Class

To create a class

1. Click on the + button at the right upper corner of the screen.

2. A little menu will appear. In that menu, click on "create a class." You will be required to fill in some details concerning yourself and the class you want to create. Be sure to choose a good class name and section. Preferably, let the class name be the title of your class. This is important as it will help you locate the class easily.

3. When you are done with all those, click "create" and wait for your class to be created.

Personalizing a Class

We discussed in earlier sections of this book that one of the major benefits of using the Google Classroom tool is that it allows you some amount of autonomy as the teacher and you get to personalize and design your classroom in such a way that is appealing to you and the students. These are a few things you can do to personalize your Google Classroom;

Selecting a theme for your classroom

The Classroom has a number of themes you can select from and toggle in a bid to customize your experience and make it more fun. This is how you can change themes;

1. Inasmuch as the classroom has a number of themes that you can make use of at any time, this is your opportunity to get creative. Remember that we talked about making the experience personal for yourself and fun for the students, right? This is where you get to make that happen.

2. You can create your theme in such a way that it relates to what the class is about and to the topic you are going to be discussing during the sessions.

3. The image you use as a banner image (top frame) in your classroom has to be at least 800x200 pixels in size. There is a lot of space there, so you need a rectangular image that big to cover up the space. This, however, does not mean that you cannot get to make use of smaller images. Smaller images can be used, but they will not fill up that space, and they may leave that spot looking unkempt.

4. When you have found the image that you will want to use, download/save it to the images folder on your device.

5. From the images you have downloaded to your device, you can set a class banner for your classroom.

6. Click on "select a photo from your computer," and select the picture you want to make use of from your device's memory. This is what it looks like

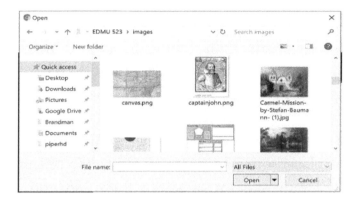

7. When the image you want to use opens up, size it accordingly and select the part of the picture that will be more appropriate for the banner of your classroom.

8. When you have done this, click on "select class theme" and wait for the new theme to be put in place.

Gallery

Upload

Upload ▸ bunker_hill.jpg

To crop this image, drag the region below and then click "Select class theme"

Select class theme   Cancel

9. You also have the options of changing the color patterns in your classroom as this will help with the personalization.

Navigating Google Classroom

1. Once you have signed in and created the class, click on the class name to open it up.

2. Navigating is easy because all you have to do is to click a tab at the top of the page so that you can jump to a section of the classroom.

These are the options available;

A. Stream; is a central point of convergence. This is the spot from where you can view all the class posts, announcements, and every other thing in-between. When a new unit is added to classwork, it automatically appears on the stream. Toward the left side of the stream, you will see an area where all the upcoming activities are detailed; upcoming assignments and their due dates. This helps you to keep tabs of what is going on in the classroom without having to move around a lot.

B. Classwork; from this tab, you are able to create assignments, questions and other class materials. As a hack to keep the classwork page organized, you can create topics under which you can group the classwork and other related materials that you instruct your students with.

C. People; under this tab, you can take inventory of all your students and keep track of them. Here, you can find the class roster, and also a list of all the class teachers and those that have a role to play in the class. In this tab, you can also add more people to your class.

D. Grades; From here, you can access submitted assignments, grade them and return them to the students for them to have a look at their performances as well. This interface allows you to see the individual scores of the students and the class average at the same time.

This is how the interface from where you can access all these options looks like;

3. To return to the classroom home screen, click the menu button at the top left corner of your screen. The menu button is those three lines at the top of the screen.

4. A dropdown menu will appear once you have clicked the button, from this menu, select **classes**. This will take you back to the main screen where you will see all the classes you are a part of. To access any other class, all you need to do is click on it, and you will gain access to the class.

Adding Students to Your Classroom

As the teacher, you have the ability to add students to your classroom and there are a number of ways you can get that done. In this section of the book, we will walk you through how you can be able to add students to your Google Classroom.

Adding students via email

For this to work out, your students MUST have a Gmail or a Google email address. So, if you are going to make use of this option, please make sure that they have all these in place. To invite students,

1. Log into your class and click on the "students" tab at the top of the screen.

2. When you have done this, a drop-down box will appear. From this box, click on "invite."

3. In the "select students to invite" dialogue box, you will see a list of students that you can invite to the classroom. Note that this list opens up from the list of students you have from either the school's directory, your personal contacts, or a group list. Check the box(es) next to the name(s) of the student(s) you want to invite to class.

4. When you are satisfied that you have selected all the students you want to invite to class, click on the "invite students" button at the bottom of the page. The class list will update to include the students you just invited to the class.

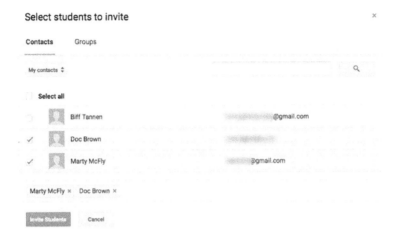

At their end(s), the student(s) you invited will receive emails saying that they have been invited to join the class. The emails will come with links in it and each student has to click on the link in the mail to be granted access to the class.

Adding students via access codes

Instead of having to invite all the students by yourself, you can permit them to let themselves in using the access codes to the class. Here's how you let them do just that.

1. Open up your class and get the class code. The class codes are usually located at the bottom left part of the screen.

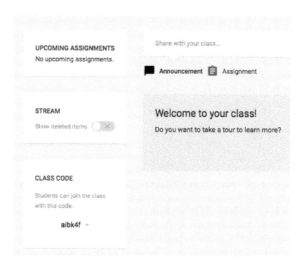

2. Making use of the most convenient ways of reaching them, give the access codes to your students. You can choose to send the codes as emails or whatever works for all of you.

3. Instruct the students to visit the Google Classroom's official website at classroom.google.com. Tell them to click the plus sign at the top right corner of their screen after which they can type in the code they have gotten and get instant access to the class.

Creating Assignments and Materials

Creating an Assignment

Creating an assignment in the Google Classroom is a simple task. All you need to do is follow these steps;

1. Go to the official website at classroom.google.com

2. From the dashboard, click the class you want to access and wait for it to open up.

3. At the top of the classroom page that has opened, you will see a "create" button. This button opens up to a lot of features but for the sake of what we are looking at here, click "assignment" after the drop-down box has appeared.

4. When you have done this, enter the title of the assignment you want to create, alongside any other piece of information that is vital to the assignment.

5. You can go further with the creation and editing of the assignment. When you have included all the details that need to be in it, you can go ahead to

publish it so that all your students can access the assignments.

Using Google Docs with Assignments

When creating assignments for your students, there may be times that you will need to attach Google Docs files to the assignments. This may be as a result of needing to communicate instructions in clearer terms or maybe because the assignments are lengthy and they will have to be done in details. This, however, should not be a problem for you because following these few steps, you should be able to pull this off.

1. Create the file you want to attach to the assignment. This should contain the extra details you are looking to get across to the students. Package this in a Google Docs file. This is what you will be working with.

2. When you are about to attach the extra file you have created (docs file), be sure to choose the correct setting so that your students can interact with them the way you want them to. When you have attached

a file to an assignment, you will find a dropdown menu with these options;

A. Students can view file; if you select this option, you are allowing your students to have access to the content of the attached file. They can only see it, but can not edit it or have any other form of interaction with the document.

B. Students can edit file; use this option if you are attaching a file that you want your students to be able to edit or directly make changes to in response to the questions asked. This will be very beneficial if you are looking to get the students to collaborate on a project or at least, fill out something on the document.

C. Make a copy for each student; this command allows multiple copies of the document you are uploading to be made. One copy will be sent to each student's assignment tab and they will not be able to access any copy that is not theirs. This is a great option to use if you are looking to get them to work individually and submit their assignments to you one by one.

Using topics

Topics allow you to sort and group your assignments in such a way that promotes ease of access. With topics, you are able to arrange documents and class materials in a way that you do not have to go through a million documents and files all in search of one. If used well, this feature will save you a lot of time and energy.

This is how you use topics in the Google Classroom.

1. On the classwork tab, you can make edits and choose topics to sort and group your assignments and teaching materials into.

2. To create a topic, click on the "create" button which is at the top of the classroom dashboard. A drop-down box will appear.

3. From this drop-down box, click on "topic." When you have done this, go ahead to add the topic details and begin to group the materials based on the topics you have created.

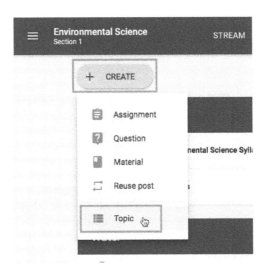

Using Google Forms with Google Classroom

Google Forms allows you to create quizzes and surveys in the classroom. This is one great way for you to request for feedback from the students, or obtain information that you can compare and use to make the experience better.

Creating a Quiz

This is how you use Google forms to create a quiz in your classroom.

1. You need to start out by creating a basic form. To create a basic form, go over to the Google forms homepage so that you can get started.

    A. On the homepage, click on the "blank" icon to get started with creating a new form.

    B. Before getting started with customizing the form, you need to start out by making certain changes to the format of the form. To get started with this, click the "settings" icon in the top-right corner of the forms tab.

C. Clicking this button will open up a new page for you. At the top of the page, you will see a series of text. Click on "quizzes" and toggle the "make this a quiz switch" pop up. When you have done this, a few quiz options will come up for you to be able to control how your students will be able to interact with the quiz you are about to send out to them.

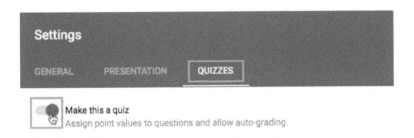

D. Once you are done with choosing the right form you want the form to appear to your students in, go ahead and click on "save."

E. Name the form, then get started with writing the questions that you want the students to answer. Remember that the form comes with a few options that allow you to be able to customize it so that you can get the best experience for your students. You can change the fonts and the colors of your forms.

2. When you are done creating the form, you need to go ahead and make sure that you have selected the right answers to the questions asked. This will help you save more time as it allows the system to automatically grade the students. To select the right answer for each question you create, simply click on "answer key." The screen appears differently depending on the types of questions you have chosen.

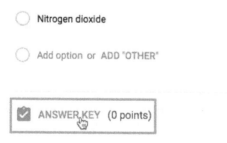

A. For a multiple-choice question, you can simply tick the correct answer in the answer box.

B. For questions that require short answers, you will find a field marked as "add a correct answer." All you need to do is type the correct answer. If the answer requires that the student will write a few words, you can write a few different answers, which are all variants of the real answer. This will give the system options to select from seeing as people think differently and not all your students will write the same thing in the same way. This is what the field looks like;

What term is defined as "the settling of substances at the bottom of a liquid"?

0 : points

Sedimentation ✕

Sediment ✕

Add a correct answer

☐ Mark all other answers incorrect

C. For questions that require a paragraph answer, you do not always get the chance to put in the right answer. This is because the answers that will come to these questions are usually longer and will always be framed in different ways by different students. For these questions, you will have to read through them and grade them by yourself.

3. When you are done selecting the answers, move on to select how many points will be attached to each question.

4. If you think it to be necessary, you can attach answer feedback to each of the questions. This is basically where you get to type in a little paragraph text that will serve as some form of explanation that will show up depending on whether or not the student gets the question right. In this section, you can choose if the feedback will appear when the student has entered a correct answer or an incorrect answer.

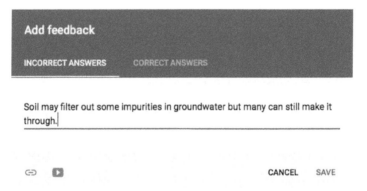

5. When you have gone through all the motions for all the questions you have included in the form, you can go on to preview the form. This act allows you to take a look at the finished work of the form you have created. This way, you get to see what the students will be seeing when they have started interacting with the form. If there are errors in the forms, you can go ahead to edit them and make changes where necessary.

Creating a Timed Quiz in Google Classroom

If you want to be able to correctly assess how well your students were able to understand a concept, you may want to test them with a timed quiz. Just as the name implies, timed quizzes are a great way to get your students to answer questions from their heads and not go out to Google answers. In a nutshell, you attach a timer that begins to read once the student opens up the quiz and when the timer runs out, he loses access to the document. Creating a timed quiz is not too difficult, but you will need to make use of some extra tools like plugins to make this work seeing as the feature is not included in the default Google Classroom.

Here are the steps to get you to where you are going.

1. Install the application that can help you create this quiz. For the sake of this example, we will be making use of iSpring QuizMaker. To get started, look up this tool either on your web browser or on your android / iOS app and make sure that it is installed on the device that you want to create the quiz on.

2. Open the tool you have downloaded and click on "graded quiz." You will find this on the left side of the screen once you have launched the application.

3. Choose the type of question you want to include in the quiz. Once you click on the graded quiz button, you will see that there are 14 question types that you

can choose from in this tool. It is imperative that you choose one type of question so that you can move on to the next stage of the process.

4. When you have chosen the question type, input the question text. In the picture that has been inserted below, you will see that the question type chosen was multiple-choice questions. Fill in this section by entering the text of your question in the question text bar and the answer options in the choices section. Signify that option is the correct answer by marking it with a dot (checking it as the correct answer).

Multiple Choice Question

During a breathing task for infants, you should

Choices

Correct	Choice	
○	Place a mouth over an infants's mouth	×
◉	Place a mouth over an infants's mouth and nose	×
○	Place a mouth over an infants's nose	×
	Type to add a new choice	

Feedback and Branching

	Feedback			Branching	Score
Correct:	That's right! You chose the correct response.		···	→	10
Incorrect:	During a breathing task for infants, you should place a mouth		···	→	0

5. Set the timer. In this tool we are examining, there are different ways for you to set a timer for the quiz;

A. Set the same time for all questions.

This way, all questions have the same time allotted to answering them. At the end of the time set for one question, the next one pops up. Use this option if all the questions on the quiz are of the same difficulty level and there are no questions that require extra time for thinking and brainstorming.

To use this method for your timed quiz, click on properties in the toolbar of the software. The button has been highlighted in the image below.

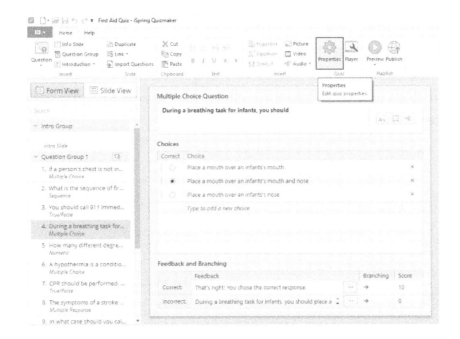

Select the "question properties" tab from the options that will pop up in the next screen.

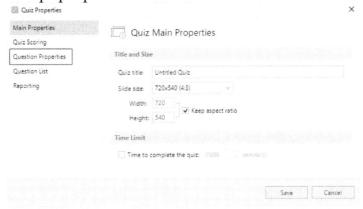

In the time limit section of the page, click on "limit time to answer question." When you have done this, set a time limit to effect in all of the questions that you have added to the form, and click on "save" to apply the settings to the form.

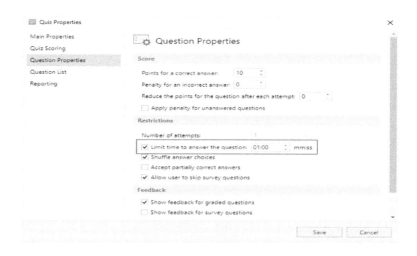

B. Set different time limits for the questions.

Depending on the kind of quiz you have set for your students, they may need different time limits to answer different questions. Some questions will be more difficult than the others and the goal of making use of this kind of timers for the quiz is to make sure that they have enough time to answer all the questions asked without feeling as though they had too much time for one question and not enough time for the other.

To get this timer activated for the quiz, all you need to do is select the questions one after the other and in the slide options tab, click on "limit time to answer the question." When you have clicked on this tab, set the time for the question and repeat the process for all the questions that form the quiz.

C. Set a general time limit

You can set an overall time allotted for the quiz. This does not regulate the amount of time the student spends on each question. It just makes sure that when the timer reads zero, they do not have access to the quiz again. To set up this kind of timer,

1. Click on "properties."
2. In the main properties tab, select "time to complete the quiz." Click on "save" to apply the changes you have set to the quiz. Be sure that the time you allocate for the completion of the quiz is enough time for your students to go through it successfully. If this is not the case, you may end up having a wrong assessment for the students without knowing that they just did not have enough time to go through the quiz.

Selecting the Right Answers For Your Questions

We have touched a bit on this in an earlier section but for the sake of making it stick once again, we are going to go over how you can be able to select the right answers to the questions you add in the Google Classroom.

1. Start by creating a quiz using Google forms. You will find a detailed how-to guide in one of the earlier sections of this chapter).
2. To activate this feature, you will have to define the correct answer for each of the questions in the assignment/the forms you are sending out to your students. To activate this, click on the "answer key" directly below the questions you have just inserted.

3. Depending on the type of questions and the answers they require, different screens will appear after you have struck this button. Here is a quick rundown of what you will find once you have clicked on the button.

A. With questions that demand that the student click a check-box (multiple-choice question), all you need to do is simply select the answer from the list of options you have provided. At this point, you should have something of this nature

Which chemical compound can cause acid rain?

○ Hydrogen dioxide

○ Carbon dioxide

◉ Sulfur dioxide

○ Nitrogen dioxide

B. For questions that have a short answer attached to them (maybe anywhere from one word to a few words long), enter the answer in the answer space provided under the question. Just to make sure that many students as possible are given the opportunity to get the correct answer, you may want to enter as many variants of the answer as you probably can. This way, even those that enter in the answer with a few different words can still have the opportunity to be graded correctly. For answers that don't match the answers you have provided, the system automatically grades them as being wrong. When creating answers to these kinds of questions, if you tick the box next to the "mark all other answers incorrect," the system will automatically mark any other answer that is not presented the same way you gave yours wrong. If you leave the box unmarked, answers that are not the same as the one you have will be left unattended and you will have to check them up by yourself.

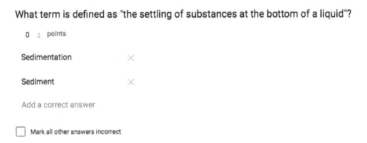

C. When you are asking a question that demands that the student gives a long answer that is up to a paragraph or even more than that, you do not get the chance to preload answers into the system. For this kind of questions, you need to go through the answers that your students give and grade them manually.

Adding Sections to Your Quiz

Using the forms option, you do not only get to create quizzes but you can also add sections to your quizzes. Depending on how long the quiz will be, you may want to group everything according to different sections so that different sections can come up in different pages, instead of trying to get the whole thing to be stuffed into one page. This is exactly how you can get that done.

1. To add sections to your quiz, simply click the "add section" icon in the toolbar on the side of the page. When your section is created, you can go through the same process detailed in the earlier section to add questions to the section. Also bear in mind that you can move questions across sections until you are ready to publish the form you have created in the classroom it was meant for.

Adding Quizzes to Classes

Now that you are done with creating your quiz, it is time to add it to the class you meant for it to be available to.

1. When you are done with creating the quiz and the form is ready, it is time for you to bring it over to your classroom. Bear in mind that there is no magic to this as it is simply almost like how you can insert the Google Docs in the classroom. All you need to do is start creating a new assignment in the classroom.

2. When creating the assignment, click on the Google drive icon that is in the lower-left corner of the screen. The quiz you created earlier usually gets backed up to the cloud and is saved to your Google drive. All you need to do is locate it from here and insert it into the assignment you are creating.

3. Select the quiz you want to insert, and click on "add." This includes the quiz in the assignment which you can send off for your students to work on.

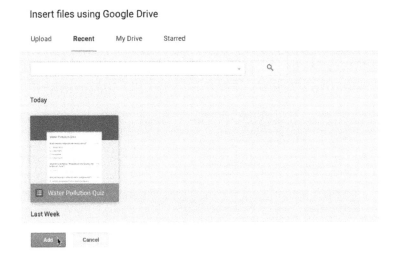

Grading and Leaving Feedback

When you are done with creating the quiz for your students, it is expected that they go through the quiz and hand it over to you for analysis and feedback. It is vital that you know how to grade your quiz and how to leave feedback for the students in your classroom. There are a few ways you can get this done.

Viewing Individual Assignments

1. To view assignments in this mode, you need to start by navigating to the classwork tab. When the tab has opened, find the assignment you would want to grade and click on it to open up the assignment.

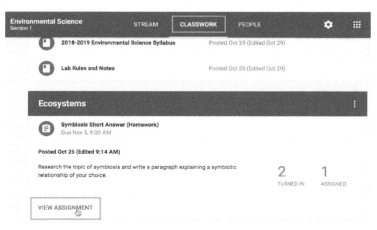

2. Clicking on the view assignment tab at the bottom of the page will open up the student's work page for the assignment. It is on this page that you will be able to see in detail what each student has been up to and be able to grade them based on their performances.

3. To grade performances from the work page, all you need to do is to click the score next to each student's name and insert the score you would like to award to that student. When you are done with inserting

the student's score, click on "return" to publish the result so that the student can see his score for the quiz you have just graded.

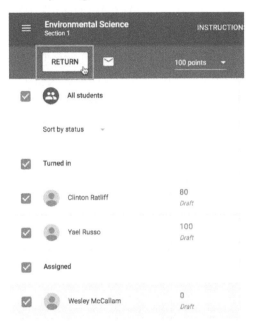

Grading Assignments Using the Grading Tool.

With this option, you can grade each assignment using the grading tool that is within each assignment turned in by each student. This is how you can get started with this option.

1. Click on an assignment you want to grade and allow it to open. At the right side of the screen, you will see the grading tool as it is featured in a column. In this

column, there is a "grade" field. In this field, you can insert the grade you want to assign for each assignment by typing it in manually. If you would love to, you can also leave feedback for the students so that they have something to build on when reviewing their performances. If you are going to leave feedback, you can do this using the "private comments" field. This will make sure that it is only the student that has the work you are grading that will be able to access the feedback you have given.

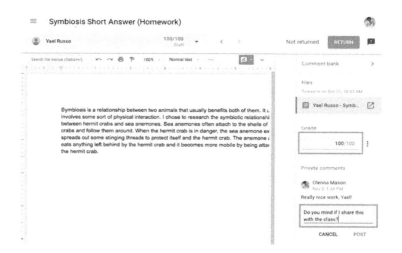

2. When you are done with grading the entire assignment and are satisfied with what you have

done, you can go ahead to release the result to the student by hitting the "return" button.

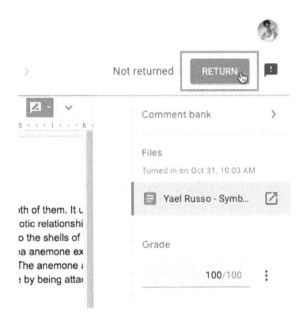

Viewing Class Grades as a Whole

One of the amazing features of the Google Classroom tool is that it allows you the luxury of exporting class grades directly from your classroom to Google spreadsheets. With spreadsheets, you are able to compare data at a glance and have access to valuable insights from what you have compiled.

Spreadsheets have the unique feature of showing you the grades for each assignment turned in by each student. Coupled with this insight also is the assignment's average grade and you can also see the class' average grade as a whole, just with one glance.

To export the grades you have compiled, all you need to do is

1. Go to the work page of any of the students in your class. Click the "gear" icon at the top right-hand side of the page. A drop-down box will appear with a few options.

2. From the options that appear, click on "copy all grades to Google sheets."

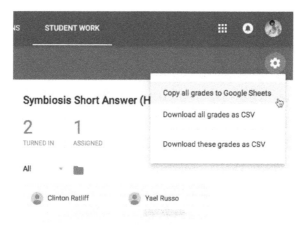

3. Note that clicking on the option in the point above will not automatically update the spreadsheet that has been created. This implies that whenever you are done with grading other assignments, you will have to export them manually because you will not find them in the spreadsheet if you do not remember to keep this on top of your mind.

Communicating with Students and Parents

To a very large extent, you have interacted with the students in your class and you have come to see exactly how well off they are in their performances. The next step is for you to find a way to establish a communication line with the students and their parents if this becomes necessary.

This is necessary so that you can get to plug as many holes as can be plugged with the student's academic endeavors and also keep the parents in the loop as to how well their child is performing. Communicating with the students and their parents can be achieved through a number of means including;

Emailing Your Students

Here are a few things to take note of before you begin with this process.

1. Note that you can send your students emails from the classroom using the classroom account

2. If you are using an account that was set up for the school, the administrator has to give you permission to email students and other people using the classroom account by turning on Gmail for both yourself and the students to be able to communicate with. If this is not done, all forms of communication will be limited to just the classroom space.

3. You can only email up to 100 students at the same time. If you have more than 10o students and you need to pass some kind of information across to them, you need to break them into batches of at most 100 emails per batch.

4. Parents must not have a Gmail account to be able to receive and interact with the emails you want to send them from the classroom. They need to have an

email account (no doubt), but it does not really matter who is their service provider.

To email your students using a computer

1. Go to the official website at classroom.google.com

2. Click the class from where you want to email your students and when the class has opened up, click on the "people" tab at the top of the screen.

3. If you want to

A. Email one student,

I. Find the student's name from the list of students in the class.

II. Next to his name, you will see a "more" button. Click on this button.

III. Click on "email student" afterwards. Construct your email and send to him.

B. Email many students at the same time,

I. Check the boxes next to the names of all the students you want to email at the same time.

II. At the top of the page, click the "actions" button.

76

III. When you have done these, click "email students." Construct and send the emails you want them to receive.

C. Email the whole class,

I. Open up the class list. Next to the "actions" tab, you will find a box. Check this box, then click the "actions" button.

II. Click "email students." Remember that you can only mail 100 students per time. If there are more than this number in your class, please be sure to get this done in batches of at most 100 students.

To email your students using an android device

1. From the application you have installed on your device, open the classroom from where you want to send a mail to your students.

2. At the bottom of the screen, you will find the "people" tab. Tap on this to open up the tab.

3. To email a student, tap the "more" button next to the student's name and tap on "email student." you can go

ahead to construct and send the email you wish to send to the student after you have done this. Note that you can also attach files in the mail you are sending. To do this, find and click on "send attachments with your Gmail message." This tool will help you send other file types like documents, PDFs, images, etc. alongside the mail you are sending.

Remember to also include a topic for your mail. This way, the students can see that it is something serious that needs their attention. With this in place, they are more likely to attend to the mails faster than they would have if you had just sent it in that way, without adding a topic to the mail.

To email your students using an apple device (iPhone or iPad)

1. Make sure that the Gmail and the Classroom apps are installed on your device before you get started.

2. When you have done this, tap on the class you want to access and tap the "people" icon at the bottom of your screen.

3. To email a student, find the student's name and click on the "more" icon next to it. A list of options will show up. From that list, select "email student." Construct and send your mail bearing in mind the best practices that have been discussed in the section above.

4. To email more than one student, tick the boxes next to the names of the students you want to mail and go through the motions of sending the mails to them. Just make sure that you are not sending the mail to more than 100 students per time.

Posting Announcements in the Classroom

In the main class stream, you can schedule and post announcements for your students. Announcements are posts that do not have assignments attached to them.

They are usually a means of communicating something vital that the students should be aware of in the classroom - maybe a reminder of due dates, that there will be a quiz/test coming up, and all the rest of them.

To create announcements, follow the guides below this section of the book.

Posting announcements using your android phone

1. Launch the classroom app and open up the class you want to post the announcement to.

2. On that page, you will see an option that allows you to "share with the class." Tap on this option and create the announcement you want the class to see.

3. You can also post announcements to multiple classes at the same time. Note, however, that announcements that are made to multiple classes will be seen by all the students in all those classes. To do this, tap "share with your class" from the stream page.

4. This will open up to you a list of the classes you have created as the teacher. Seek out the classes you want to post the announcement to and tap "next."

5. Tap any additional classes you want to receive the announcement and when you have done this, tap "done." This will make sure that all the classes receive the announcements you have sent to them.

Posting announcements using your computer

1. Using your Chrome browser, visit classroom.google.com

2. On the stream page, click on "share something with your class" and enter the announcements you wish to share.

3. If you are looking to make the announcement to more than one class at the same time, on the stream page, select "share something with my class."

4. Next to "for," you will see an arrow that points downwards. This arrow signifies that there are other options hidden within that drop-down menu and to access them, all you have to do is click on it. After clicking on the arrow, select the classes that you want to receive the announcements.

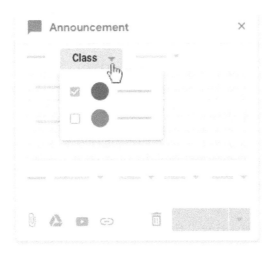

Note that posting announcements to your classes if you are making use of an apple device (iPad and iPhone) is pretty much the same process as with that of the android devices. Just log into your Google Classroom account and follow all the steps that were outlined in that section of this book above.

Class Summaries For Parents

Class summaries for parents is a great way for the parent/guardian of the student to be able to keep tabs with what the child has been up to in the classroom and know whether or not he is doing well with his academics. Email summaries give you an overview of what has been done in the classroom and can allow the parent have an idea of what the student is learning. It, however, does not contain the grades the student gets in class. To get access to these data, the parent has to communicate with the teacher to send it over or ask the student straight up.

Here's a rundown of the details that are included in the parent's email summary.

- Class activities; this allows the parent to have insight into what is going on in the classroom. He sees the announcements, assignments, and questions directly posted by the teachers.

- Missing work insight allows the parent to know when his child does not turn in the work he was supposed to turn in for any reason.

- Upcoming work shows the time that assignments and tests are due to hold. This way, the parent can play a more involved role in his child's academic success.

Class email summaries allow the parent to play a more involved role in the student's learning process. For this to work, however, the parent and the instructor have to work together (in the sense that the parent has to be willing to follow up on the student's progress as much as the teacher is willing to let him have access to all the necessary data that can grant him insight into how well his child is doing). As the parent, you can have class summaries emailed to you and if you have an active Gmail account, you can change how frequently you receive these messages, update your time zone and better optimized to be more in touch with the activities of your child in the classroom. These do not mean that you will be unnecessarily bugged with emails from the classroom. You can choose to unsubscribe from receiving those emails. If for some reason, you don't want to get emails from the classroom anymore, you can unsubscribe, but your email will still be connected to your child's classroom account.

To get email summaries of your child's activities in the classroom,

1. Ask the teacher/administrator of the school (depending on the type of account the trainers are using for the classroom) to email you an invitation to join the class.

2. When you receive this email, open it up and read through the terms of service. Those will better get you equipped for what you are about to get started with. When you are done with doing that, click on "accept' at the bottom of the screen. If you are not the legal guardian of the student, be sure to indicate this by selecting the "I am not the guardian" option lying next to the "accept" button.

3. Click "accept."

4. To unsubscribe from the email summaries at any time, hit the "unsubscribe" button at the bottom of each mail you receive. If you do not have a Google account, this action will remove you as the guardian from the student you were interested in.

5. You can remove yourself from the student's account at any time. This action separates you entirely from the account of the student and you will no more be able to monitor his progress. To do this, all you need to do is

I. Click "settings" at the bottom of each of the summary emails you receive. This button is not hard to find as it is just at the lower part of the screen once you open up any of the messages in your mailbox.

II. When you have clicked settings, the name of the student you are connected to in the classroom will appear. Next to the student's name, you will find a trash icon which is like a bin. Click this icon to remove yourself from the student's account.

Students' Guide

Joining a class

If you must have access to a class, you must be signed into Chrome with your student credentials; the same account that you used to sign up for Google Classroom. As a student, there are a number of ways through which you can gain access into a class, including making use of the class code as given to you by the teacher or accessing the class through a link.

This is how you can gain access into a class as a student.

Accessing a class via class code

1. Start off by signing into Google Chrome. This is really simple to do. If you are using a new device, the first time you launch the Chrome browser, you will be asked

to log into your Gmail account. Make sure the details (email and password) you enter at this point are the same details you used to sign up for Google Classroom. This way, you do not have to worry a lot about navigating another way.

2. If you are using an older device and you need to sign into the Chrome account you used to register for classroom, just launch the application.

3. Open up a new tab to access the sign-in menu. When you have done this, enter in the details that you used to register for classroom and click next" at the bottom of the page.

4. When you have signed in to Chrome, go to the official website at classroom.google.com

5. This will open up a page where you will get the option to join or create a class. You access these options by clicking the + sign at the top right corner of the page you have visited.

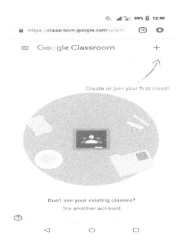

6. Because you are a student, it is not your job to create a class so all you need to do is click on "join a class." when you have done this, you will see a note that will tell you to get the class code from the teacher and enter it into a blank field on the screen. Do just that and enter your class code into the field that has been provided.

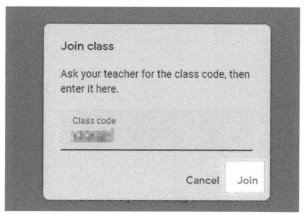

7. Enter the class code provided by your teacher and click "join."

Accessing a class via teacher's invite

If your teacher is to invite you to a class via email, you will see that there will be an access code in the email. If you are to join a class using this method, all you need to do so is contained in the mail you received from your teacher. Follow these steps to join.

1. To join from your computer, open up the mail you received and click on the link in the mail.

2. Select the account you use for classroom and click on "join." Wait to be taken to the class.

3. The processes are the same whether you are joining the class with an Android phone, iPhone or iPad. Click the link in the mail you received, make sure you are logged into the correct account and click "join.

Accessing Assignments and Posting Comments Via the Stream

From your computer
This is how you can see assignments that you have to get done in the classroom

1. Visit the official website at classroom.google.com

2. On the class card, you can see the next three assignments that you have to get done, as far as they all fall within the next week.

3. Click on an assignment to see all the details that are contained within it.

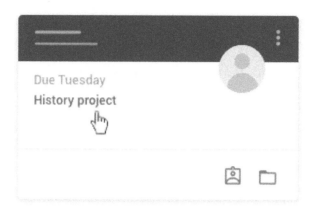

From your android device

1. Open the classroom app.

2. On the class card, you will see a list of upcoming assignments and other relevant classwork and announcements.

3. Tap on a class card to see the rest of the assignments and other valuable information that relates to the work at hand.

4. The process is the same for you, even if you are using an Apple device like your iPhone or iPad.

Viewing a List of All Assignments

You can see all the assignments that have been given for a class at the same time

From your phone

1. In the classroom app, tap on "to-do list" at the top of the screen. This will open up to you a list of projects that need your attention all grouped together by category.

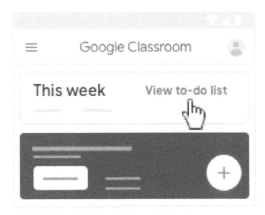

2. When you have done this, a screen will appear. From that screen, select the category of projects you want to take a look at (in this case, you will tap the "assigned" tab).

3. Tap on any of the titles that pop up to see the details and instructions attached to the assignment.

From your computer

1. Go to the official website of Google Classroom.

2. You will see a list of all your class cards in front of you. On a class card you access, click on your work. It is the little icon that has the figure of a person that is attached to the class cards.

3. Conversely, you can choose to click on the class to open it up. Then click on "classwork" and "view your work."

4. Click on the title of the assignment to view it in details - including all attachments and instructions left by your teacher.

Using Google Classroom to View Assignment's Due Dates

1. To see the due date for an assignment, open up the classroom stream.

2. On a class card, click on "your work."

3. You will see a list of projects you have to handle and things that require your attention. To filter the answers that will pop up on your screen, take a look at the options and click on "assignments." To see more details about the assignment, click on it, and click "view details." These details include the day you are due to hand in the assignment.

Accessing Your Classroom Files in Google Drive

The Google Classroom has been described as a paperless tool because you do not get to do anything with physical books and pens. One of the ways this is achieved is through the incorporation of the Google drive into the classroom. The best part of the classroom is that almost everything you do in the classroom is automatically saved to the cloud and this greatly reduces the chances of having lost documents and important class details getting missing. When you log into the classroom for the first time, a folder is automatically created in the cloud (Google drive) for the work you will be doing in that classroom. As you keep up with the work you are doing, more folders are created in the classroom.

In your drive, you can access the classroom folder by following these steps.

1. Make sure you are signed into the account you used to sign up for classroom. This is the account to which all your details will automatically be backed up.

2. In the drive app (or visit drive.google.com if you are making use of a computer, or you do not have the drive app installed on your phone), locate the general classroom folder. You can do this by performing a quick search in the drive. To perform a search, click on the search bar at the top of the page and type in the

keyword you want to search for. Allow the search results to come up.

3. From the list of results you now have, be sure to find the correct folder you are looking for (because every classroom has its own folder created within the main folder). Click on the folder and it will open up for you to have access to the files within the folder.

A Short message from the Author:

Hey, I hope you are enjoying the book? I would love to hear your thoughts!

Many readers do not know how hard reviews are to come by and how much they help an author.

I would be incredibly grateful if you could take just 60 seconds to write a short review on Amazon, even if it is a few sentences!

>> Click here to leave a quick review

Thanks for the time taken to share your thoughts!

Chapter 3

Using Google Meet For Live Video Classes

What is Google Meet?

Google Meet is one of the software tools developed by the Google company. In 2019, Google began to plan to take Hangouts away from the marketplace. At the time, Hangouts was the video conferencing and meeting tool that had been developed by the Company.

In essence, Google Meet is Google's video meeting tool that allows people from different parts of the world to be able to meet at a virtual location and interact in real-time. Google Meet is compatible with android, iOS devices, and also has a web tool that can be accessed from any Chrome browser.

Why Google Meet is a Must-Have

As you should have picked up by now, Google Meet is a video conferencing tool that allows people from all around the world to have virtual meetings and interact in real-time. Here are a few reasons why Google Meet is a very vital tool for you to have;

1. It makes it possible for people to meet and interact with themselves from any area of the world in real-time, distance no longer an inhibition of this. If all the meetings you had to attend were physical, you would be restricted a lot, but with tools like these, you will meet up with a lot of stuff you would not have gotten otherwise.

2. With this tool, you have access to a lot of amazing features that can help you have powerful and very impactful meetings and training sessions. These include the ability for you to share your screen (so that those in the meeting can see what is on the screen of your device. This is a great way for your knowledge to be communicated without a lot of fuss on your part), record a meeting (so that you can have access to the details of the meeting much later on or for the people who were not able to be present to have access to what was shared), and a lot more tools that can make your video conferencing journey easier.

3. Meetings conducted with this tool are secure. All the streams that are broadcast over the internet (audio and

video) streams are encrypted. This way, you do not have to worry about what is happening to the information you are sharing and the people who will have access to them over the internet.

4. You have the liberty to try out all the attached features of this amazing tool to see for yourself all that you can potentially achieve with it. Also, for the most part, this tool is a free software so even if your establishment does not have these kinds of meetings in the budget, you can easily make use of the tool without having to break the bank.

5. You can have access to the same account, tool and meeting across different devices. As we said earlier, Google Meet supports android, iOS devices and also has a web-based version. With all these options, access is almost unlimited.

6. As an educator, you can get to chat with your students in real-time. This will foster the relationship you have with them and make the learning/teaching process more fun than it usually is.

How to estimate the number of students for Google Meet

As a teacher, Google Meet is an amazing tool for you to profit off of and reach as many students as you can reach. As said earlier, you can make use of this tool as a free user, or even as a paid user. As a free user, you are allowed to have a meeting with up to 100 participants per time. If you are using the paid version, you get to meet with up to 250 people per time.

Type of G suite account	Maximum number of students allowed for each meeting.
With a regular (non G suite account)	100
G Suite basic or G suite education account	100
G Suite essentials, G suite for business	150
G suite enterprise for Education	250

How to Set-up Google Meet Via the Homepage

To get started using Google Meet, you must have a personal Google account or a G suite account. This is the pass you need to be able to access Google Meet.

To start a meeting on Google Meet with your computer

1. Go to the official website at meet.Google.com

2. This will open you up to the homepage. From this homepage, click on "start a meeting."

3. If you want to, you can create a nickname for your meeting, after which you click "continue." The meeting will be created and a link will be generated for you to invite your students to the meeting with.

To start a meeting with your android/apple devices

1. Install the meet app in your device (if you do not already have it). To get the application, all you need to do is go to the Google Play Store in your device (if you are using an android device) or the app store (if you are using an iOS device). Search up and install the application.

2. Open the meet app you have installed and sign into the application using the details you used to get set up in Google Classroom.

3. Tap the + sign to start up a new meeting from the device. Follow the simple prompts that will come up on your screen (to enter the nickname of the meeting if you want to), and click on "join meeting" when you are done with this.

How to Invite Students to Your Class Via Meet Homepage

When you have created a meeting, it is time to invite the participants of the meeting to come and take part in what is going on. In this case, the participants are the students that should be in the meeting. Inviting them is very simple. All you need to do is follow these steps outlined below this section of the book.

Adding People to Your Meeting

From your android phone

This feature is only available to those that are making use of a G suite account for their establishments. Also, this feature is supported by specific countries and regions for free calls to the U.S and Canada. To add someone to a meeting,

1. Tap on "information." This will make available to you the details of the meeting you have created, including the meeting link that was generated at the point when the meeting was created. You will find the information icon to be a small "i" inside a circle and it most time lies at the top of the page, next to the meeting name.

2. Tap "share."

3. Choose how you want to share the meeting details for the participants of the mail (available options are text and mail). Choose the channel that you know is most accessible for them so that they do not miss out on this important memo. The link to the meeting and dial-in numbers will open up in the text you have created to be sent as invites to the participants of the meetings.

From your computer

1. After you have created the meeting and joined it, click on the people icon at the top right side of the

screen. This icon usually is in the shape of two people with one partly behind the other. Clicking this icon expands the side panel of the meet interface.

2. Click on "add people."

3. Click "call." Select the country which your participant is to plug in the country code. After doing this, enter the person's phone number and click the dial icon.

4. When the person answers the phone, they join the meeting.

How to Use Google Meet in Google Classroom

When combined, these two tools can give you a blend of options that makes the learning/teaching experience quite comprehensive and you can be able to achieve a lot as a teacher or as an instructor teaching students from across the world. This, however, does not mean that these tools cannot be used independently of each other. You can choose to use Google Meet alone, or Google Classroom alone, but blending them together gives you more options to choose from.

To achieve this, follow these steps;

1. Generate a Google Meet link in the Google Classroom.

The easiest way you can get this done as a teacher is to generate the link in the class stream. To do this, follow these steps,

A. Go to the classroom class where you want to create a meeting.

B. From the header of the class you have accessed, click on the "generate meeting link" shown.

C. A pop-up box will appear after you have clicked this. In the box, click on the "generate meeting link" button to generate a link for the meeting you created. Click "save" once you are done. This link is going to be seen every time in your class header and you can choose to copy it so that you can send it out to the students.

2. Once you have created the link, it is time for you to invite the students to the meeting using the link you have created. To achieve this, here are a few options for you to try out;

A. Copy and paste the link in any location of the classroom where you are sure the students will see it.

Most preferably, you can add it up as an announcement.

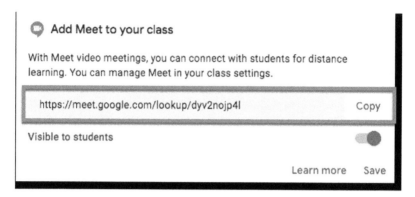

B. You can choose to toggle the visibility of the link in the classroom header. Doing this will make the link visible for the students in the classroom header. Depending on your needs, you can toggle this off and on.

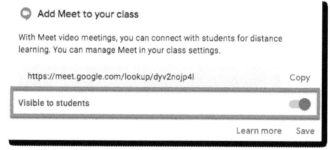

If you have chosen the above option, all the students have to do is click on the link to open the meeting you have created. The topic of the classroom will be in bold at the top of the class stream and underneath it will be the link to the meeting you have toggled for them to see. This way, all you need to do is inform them of when they will need to be present for a meeting and on their end, they will click the link to gain instant access to the meeting. This is what it should look like on their end;

To avoid unauthorized access to meeting venues, it is the best practice for you to keep the meeting link hidden from the students until it is needed. When the time is right, announce the meeting link in a post on the class stream. This way, students only gain access to a meeting that you have created and that is supervised by you.

3. When it is time for you to start the meeting, click on the meeting link on the stream page of the said class and the meeting will automatically start. Note that the meeting will not officially start until you have joined the meeting as the teacher.

How to Share Your Screen with Your Students

During the meeting you have created for your students, you can choose to share your screen with them. This way, they get to see whatever is on the screen of your computer/device per time and this makes the instructing process better for all of you.

To do this with your computer

1. Join a video meeting you have created.

2. In the bottom right corner of your screen, click the "present now" button. This automatically gets you to start the presentation. After selecting this, you will see a list of options to share your entire screen, a Chrome tab or just a window that is open on your browser.

3. Select the screen you would love to share from and click on "share." This takes your screen live so that all the students in the meeting can see it.

From your mobile devices

A. Present with your android device

1. Open the meet application and select the "present screen" option in the app.

2. Join a video meeting using the application and tap on "more." You will usually find this as three dots at the top or bottom of the screen. Note that if you are using this option, everything on your screen will be seen by every participant of the meeting.

B. Present with an iOS device

1. Join a video meet.

2. From the home screen of the meeting, tap "more." You will see this as three dots at the corner of your screen.

3. Tap "share screen" option, after which you should tap on "start broadcast." Everyone in the meeting sees everything on the screen of your phone.

Taking Attendance of Your Classroom

1. Log in to classroom.google.com.

2. On the homepage, select the class you wish to take the attendance for.

3. At the top of the class stream, select the classwork tab. This is what the interface should look like

4. Click on the select tab and ask the students that join in for the class to answer a simple question that shows that they are present. Answers to questions like "are

you present?" "Are you joining the class today?" are great questions to use for this. Feel free to use variants of this question, depending on what you seek to achieve with the classroom.

5. As students answer these questions, capture their names and their responses. An easier way to get this done will be to make use of an automated tool like Google spreadsheets as a collector for these details. When you are done, you can go through the spreadsheet and take the details you wish to take.

6. Conversely, you can post questions directly to the feed and have students answer them once they have reported for class each day. Use the responses to these questions as the indicators that a student was present or otherwise. Get creative with these questions but make sure that you are doing your best to keep up with the students and their daily activities. This way, you can stay up to date with how they respond to the classes and their attendance levels.

Muting Students During a Live Session

As the teacher, you have the most authority in the classroom, even in the case of a virtual classroom setting. Your authority allows you to permit the students to speak during a live session or to disallow them. In this section of the book, we will be looking at how you can mute a student (or all the students) during a live session so as to prevent distractions.

Muting other participants' microphones will reduce the amount of noise that comes from their ends, limiting background noise and interference with the lectures/meetings going on. There is no feature in the app that allows you to mute all participants at the same time for now. To achieve this, you need to mute them one after the other. Here's how you go about this;

1. Locate the person's thumbnail in the list of the people present in the meeting.

2. Next to the thumbnail, press the "mute" button. This automatically seizes all sounds from the person's microphone.

Note, however, that for privacy reasons, you cannot unmute a person once you have muted his microphone. To undo this action, the person will have to unmute himself from his own end of the conversation. Participants that dial in with their computers can unmute themselves by clicking the unmute button at the bottom of their screens. Participants dialing in with their phones can unmute themselves by pressing *6 on their phones. It is expected that future updates to this tool will include features that allow for this action to be carried out easily.

Recording a Google Meet Video Meeting

To record a meeting, you have to be the one who started the meeting as the instructor. If you are working for a school or organization, the administrator has to enable the feature from his end so that you can be able to record meetings. Recording a meeting is pretty easy and can be done with as much as clicking a few buttons. Note, however, that this feature is available to the G suite Enterprises and G suite enterprises for education users. Here's how you go about it;

1. Open meet.google.com. Join or Start a meeting and begin your presentation.

2. To begin recording, click on the "more" button, which is the three dots at the top or the bottom of the screen.

3. Click on the "record meeting" button that will pop up in the list of options shown.

4. Wait for the recording to start. Participants of the meeting are notified that there is a recording going on, and also when the recording stops, they will know too. The recording stops automatically when everyone leaves the meeting.

5. When you are done with what you want to record in the meeting, click on the "stop recording" button from the list of options you will find when you have pressed the more button. When you have stopped the recording, it is rendered as a video that is stored on your cloud device. This process is automatic and saves to the "meet recordings" folder on the drive. To make this recording available on your local storage device, download it from the cloud and you will have it on your local drive.

Chapter 4

Must-Have Apps and Extensions For Google Classroom

As much as the Google Classroom is pretty much self-sufficient, there are applications that, when used in conjunction with it, make the experience much better. This is because those applications incorporate more advanced features than what is attainable with just the Google Classroom app, or they bring to the table other add-on features that are not included in the Classroom app. These tools make the classroom experience worthwhile for the instructors and the learners as well and generally improves the experience on the platform. Here are a few of these tools that you will find helpful and exactly what they are used for.

Additio

This tool enables the teacher to manage day-to-day classroom activities, optimize communication within the classroom. Using this tool, you can also track student's progress using its digital gradebook and planner tool that is incorporated within the application.

Aeries Students Information System

This tool helps you to track important metrics in the classroom like student's grades, attendance and more. It also helps you make the process of circulating information like announcements easier and more seamless.

AristotleInsight K12

This tool can help you teach your students how to be more tech-savvy. With this tool, you have an all-in-one-place app for classroom administration, content management, and it can also come in handy when it comes to getting feedback.

ASSISTments

This tool can help you keep tabs with your students as it alerts you when they have responded to something they were supposed to. For instance, the tool alerts you when a student has submitted an assignment, and with this, you can be able to figure out immediately when someone is skipping activities.

Book Widgets

This tool helps you make your quizzes even better as you can get to customize them and include settings that can help you automatically grade quizzes. With this tool, you save yourself time and the energy that comes with having to grade assignments one after the other.

CodeHS

This tool helps you bring the feared subject of coding to your students and the whole school at large in a way that is fun, enlightening and engaging. This tool incorporates web-based resources, interactive session recordings and other tools that can help your students adapt quickly to coding. There are also professional development tools and other teacher tools.

Classcraft

This tool helps you make the learning process more fun for yourself and the students at large. With customized effects that keep the students in a stance of collaboration where they can work together on projects, classcraft allows them to do all these at their own pace. With this tool, learning is learner-centric.

Explain everything

This tool allows the students to make use of a very interactive whiteboard interface to enhance their thinking skills and create visuals, presentations and slides that aid the learning process. Since they are more involved in their own learning process, they can get to absorb at a higher rate and the results are usually encouraging.

Chapter 5

Cool Tips and Tricks to Enhance Your Productivity in the Google Classroom

So far, this book has covered the basics of making use of Google's interactive learning space - Google Classroom. We have looked at what you must know to get started with the app and how you can make the most out of it. In addition to all that has been covered, there are still a number of tricks that you should have up your sleeves as the teacher. These will help you make the most out of your experience on the platform, and also make it more fun for your students. Here are a few of these tricks you should have at the tip of your fingers.

1. When there is an issue you consider to be important and you do not want the students to forget it, use the "move to top" feature to get them to remember it again. This feature allows the selected resource, material, or memo to be pushed to the top of the class stream. This way, they can see it again and it stays top of mind.

2. In this same category, you can choose to send them push notifications as emails. To achieve this, follow these steps;

A. Just highlight the announcement you want to remind them of, and click the checkbox at the top of the stream that shows that you are looking to make the action available to all the members of the classroom.

B. When you have done this, click "actions" at the top of the screen to open a drop-down menu. In this menu, select "email." Once you have gone through these motions, the students will receive emails in their inbox to let them know that there is something that demands their urgent attention.

3. Why make new posts from scratch when you have made a similar post before? This is only going to get you drained quickly as you will have to create new posts every time you want to do something like make an announcement or send out a reminder for a meeting. An easy way around this is to reuse posts that you have created before.

To do this,

A. Click the + button at the bottom right of your screen and click on reuse post.

B. Make the necessary adjustments required to make the new post valid and post it to the stream. This option even allows you to reuse the attachments that you used in the first post, and edit them to suit your new needs.

As a pro tip, you can create templates that you can reuse for the posts. Whatever kind of resource that you will be making use of a lot, you can create a template for it and save it in your cloud storage. This will help you save time so that once the need arises, you can pull them out and edit as you see fit.

4. You can regulate the rate at which you receive emails that come to your inbox as a result of the activities going on in the classroom. To regulate this, click the three lines button that is at the top of the classroom stream. This will open up a drop-down box and from there, you can choose to turn off email notifications from the class. Conversely, if you choose to turn these on again, go through the same process and toggle the button on.

5. The Google Classroom is a tool that is still seeing a lot of upgrades and adjustments. As a result, it is still not at its peak. If there are tools that you think can be useful in the classroom but are not there, you have two options.

A. Search online for applications and plug-ins ins that are compatible with the classroom app. Make sure that the tools you are getting contain the features you are looking to get. Plug them in and upgrade the experience. In addition to this,

B. You can also consider sending feedback to the Google team. Engineers and software developers in the team are constantly looking for ideas to make the tool better, so giving amazing and constructive feedback/ideas will be a great way to get what you want added to the application.

6. If you find yourself confused on anything in the classroom, and you have consulted extensively with this book and materials online to no avail, you may want to look out for communities of instructors and teachers that make use of this tool. Facebook groups are a great place to start as they are usually interactive forums where people can ask questions and receive

practical answers to their questions as comments under posts, threads or social media replies.

To get further insight on matters of this nature, you may want to try out these communities and resources;

A. Pinterest resources on the Google Classroom.

B. Searching these hashtags on twitter should open you up to relevant resources - *#GoogleEDU.*

C. Facebook communities of teachers and online instructors. To find these, conduct a simple search on Facebook. This should set you in the right direction.

7. Instead of having to look for numbers and words manually in a classroom, make use of a shortcut to locate it. Notwithstanding how well you arrange your class, it is bound to get scattered and full a few weeks into your class activities. Instead of having to look for resources one after the other in the classroom, you can make use of this quick shortcut to jumpstart the process.

Control + F (on a Mac computer). This command helps you to search for keywords in the classroom stream without having to go through a ton of files and folders.

8. Make good use of Google Docs. This tool allows you to integrate applications and plug-ins to make your work easier. Earlier, we established the fact that you can include Google Docs as part of the tools needed in class. In addition to that, you can also consider making use of Google Docs to create your syllabus. These are a few reasons why you can try that out;

A. You get to create a document that can be reviewed and updated easily as the year/session unfolds. If there are revisions to the syllabus, you can easily update it on the cloud.

B. Students can have access to view the document. This way, they have something to hold on to, so that they do not have to be at the mercy of the pace the whole class is going at. Some students love to read ahead of their teachers and get prepared in advance. Using this tool and making the link to the syllabus available to the students in the class stream will be a good way to encourage the students to do their due diligence too. However, it is important that you remember to make sure the document is available to the students as a "read only" document. This way, no one tampers with it as you are the only one allowed to make edits.

125

9. Create an extension of your class, maybe a different class, to be used as a place for sporting and recreational activities. One of the easiest ways to make sure that your students are having the best time in the classroom is to diversify the activities in the classroom. One way to achieve this is to incorporate other extensive activities into your classroom. A list of tools that can help you enhance the classroom experience has been given in the previous chapter. Feel free to get creative with the options and use different plug-ins to get amazing experiences for your students. Also, find creative ways to make sure that your students are more invested in the learning process. You can think of giving them badges that they can display to signify that they are doing something that is worthwhile in the classroom. This can serve as encouragement for them to be more on their toes in the class.

10. Understand the place of privacy in the classroom. Some students do not feel too comfortable talking or relating openly with their teachers in the presence of their fellow students. This may be because they are afraid of what others will say concerning some matters they have to present. One of the ways to make sure that

the privacy of your students is always protected is to make use of private commenting to discuss salient matters. If you have noticed something about a student and you would love to talk to him about it first, this is a great way to foster the trust between both of you. This does not negate the power of face-to-face interactions, but it is a great tool that can be used as a replacement for that option. Be sure to make use of this tool when you deem fit. Your student will have more respect for you when he understands that you respect his privacy and will not allow the other students to know what he is not proud of about himself.

Use this tool when you are giving feedback for assignments, and also in-between classwork. You can get started by clicking the "view assignment" tab in the class stream.

The end... almost!

Hey! We've made it to the final chapter of this book, and I hope you've enjoyed it so far.

If you have not done so yet, I would be incredibly thankful if you could take just a minute to leave a quick review on Amazon

Reviews are not easy to come by, and as an independent author with a little marketing budget, I rely on you, my readers, to leave a short review on Amazon.

Even if it is just a sentence or two!

Customer Reviews

☆☆☆☆☆ 2
5.0 out of 5 stars ▾

5 star	▨▨▨▨▨	100%
4 star		0%
3 star		0%
2 star		0%
1 star		0%

Share your thoughts with other customers

Write a customer review ⬅

See all verified purchase reviews ›

So if you really enjoyed this book, please...
>> Click here to leave a brief review on Amazon.

I truly appreciate your effort to leave your review, as it truly makes a huge difference.

Chapter 6

Google Classroom Frequently asked Questions

Here are a few FAQs that have come up time and again and their answers to them. The aim of this section is to give you answers to your questions even before they come up.

1. Who is eligible for Google Classroom.

Answer

Google Classroom is available to basically everybody. In a nutshell, here are the classifications once again;

- Organizations that use G suite for nonprofit reasons.

- Schools using G suite for education.

- Individuals that are above 13 years of age, and have a G suite account, or at least a personal Google account.

Classroom is also available to those that are disabled and constant updates are made with disabled people in mind.

2. What is the cost of using classroom?

Answer

Google Classroom is free for all users, and they access all features included in the pack

3. What is the relationship between Google Classroom and G suite for education?

Answer

Classroom is a product in the G suite for education pack. Included in the mix is Google Docs, Slides, Sheets, and other Google utility programs. Almost all these programs can be added to the classroom to give you an all-inclusive experience and foster learning

4. Does Google own the student, teacher and/or school data entered into the classroom tool?

Answer

No. Google lays no claims to the data you enter into these tools. To make sure that you experience top-level security, they have also done their best to make sure that your data is encrypted so that there won't be a loss of sensitive data. This tool is created in such a way that if the teacher, student, or school decides to leave at any time, they can delete their data from the system without having to fear whether or not it is hidden somewhere and will be used wrongly (or will get into wrong hands).

Also, your data is NEVER used for any purposes and for any other reasons that are outside the classroom.

5. Is Classroom different when I am using a school account or a personal account?

Answer

Classroom is almost the same for the two scenarios portrayed. However, those that are making use of classroom with school accounts (G suite for education accounts) have access to more features like

- Full administration of user accounts.

- Options for guardians and parents to be more involved in their children's work by receiving email summaries

  6. How can I get further help in making use of the tool?

Answer

You can access help and have all your questions answered immediately (or almost immediately).
Visit the classroom help center to get answers to your questions.

Conclusion

Education and learning systems have come a long way since the beginning of time.

The future of learning will be in the adoption of distance learning models and the inclusion of tools like the Google Classroom. As a teacher or administrator of a school, it is vital that you understand the place of making use of these tools and incorporating them as a part of your learning materials.

This book is a deep study into the Google Classroom app. You have learned how it works, the steps to getting started with this tool, other amazing tools you can add to make sure that you and your students get the best of learning/teaching experiences on this platform. It is expedient that you take the time to practice what you have learned from this guidebook.

You will find that there will be a lot of other useful information you will get as you begin to practice with the Google Classroom app. Incorporate this tool as a teacher and a school administrator and leverage on the power of the internet to take your teaching to the next level.

Don't be limited by physical borders when you can as much as get many more people to be a part of your class.